LIFE IN THE ORKNEY ISLANDS

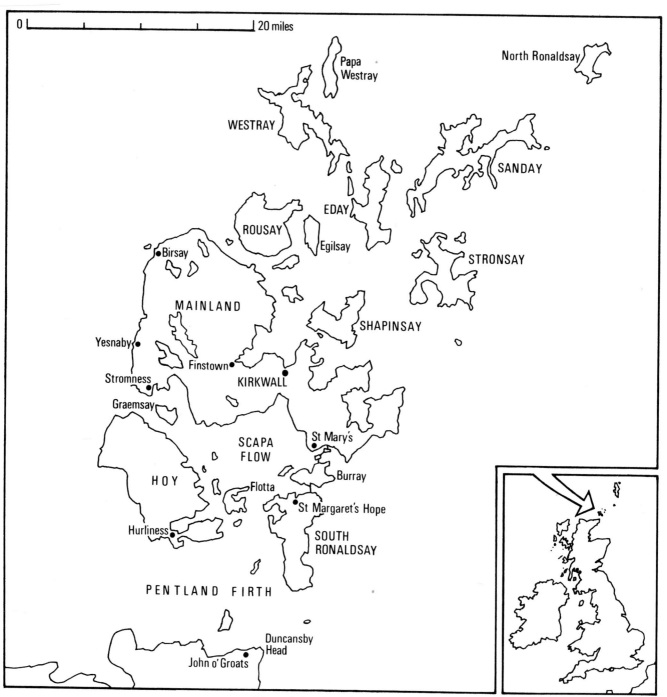

Map of the Orkney Islands.

LIFE IN THE ORKNEY ISLANDS

Photographs by Chick Chalmers

with an Introduction by Ernest W Marwick

PAUL HARRIS PUBLISHING

Edinburgh

First published in Great Britain 1979
by Paul Harris Publishing
25 London Street, Edinburgh

Reprinted 1980

© Copyright Chick Chalmers 1979

Introduction © Copyright executors of
Ernest W. Marwick

ISBN 0 904505 69 3

Printed by Bookmag, Henderson Road, Inverness

ACKNOWLEDGEMENTS

I would like to thank Bryce Wilson for his assistance and support while making the photographs and for revising the captions where it was necessary; Bob and Emily Munro without whom the task would have been much more difficult; and the Greater London Arts Association for financial assistance.

Apart from writing the introduction, Ernest Marwick gave me much encouragement and help. It was a great shock to me to learn of his death in a car accident shortly after completing ''Some Aspects of Orkney'' — the introduction to this book.

FOR HELEN

INTRODUCTION

by Ernest W Marwick

ALL AROUND the coast of the United Kingdom are islands which seem to belong naturally and geographically; which, at one time or another, have become politically identified with mainland Britain; but which still preserve differences in atmosphere, personality, and institutions.

To the far south are those portions of the ancient Dukedom of Normandy, the Channel Islands, with their French traditions and patois; to the southwest are the luxuriant, semi-tropical Scilly Islands, associated in some minds with fabled Lyonesse, in others with ruthless pirates. On the west of England is Man, governed by its Tynwald, one of the most ancient legislative assemblies in the world; while on the west of Scotland are the Celtic Hebrides: over 500 islands vastly differing in size, often as beautiful as they are rugged, and rich in Gaelic tradition, music and song.

Beyond the mountains and moors of northern Scotland, separated from it by fierce tideways where Atlantic and North Sea meet, are Orkney and Shetland. These, like Man and the Hebrides, were once part of a Norse empire. Their furthest outpost, Muckle Flugga in Shetland, is some 700 miles from London, although only 200 miles from the coast of Norway.

The present book seeks to introduce, in a series of entirely new photographs of places and people, one of these island groups, Orkney. The Orkney Islands (from 60 to 100 of them, depending on the minimum size of islet or holm you are prepared to accept as an island) are at their most southerly tip less than seven miles from John o' Groats in Caithness. They have a total area of nearly 380 square miles, and are scattered greenly, like pieces of a jig-saw on a blue table cover, over an expanse of approximately 1,600 square miles of ocean. It is thus that the visitor sees them as he flies into Kirkwall Airport from Aberdeen, Inverness or Wick. But they present a different view if he chooses to take his car to the port of Scrabster in Caithness, and parks it with many others in the hold of the m.v. *St Ola* while he tests his sea-legs on her deck.

This large car and passenger ferry-boat is based at Stromness, Orkney's western seaport. In normal weather, as she makes her way home across the Pentland Firth, the *Ola* (as she is always known) passes the west coast of Hoy, Orkney's solitary mountain island. Here the red cliffs, outlined in cool blue shadow and pierced by the dark mouths of caves, rise in places to over 1,000 feet. The tempest-scarred rampart has as its sentinel one of the best-known landmarks in Britain, the Old Man of Hoy, which was first climbed by Chris Bonnington in 1966. It is one of the many spectacular rock features which give an exciting quality to Orkney's 573 miles of coast-line.

In rougher weather, the boat may approach Stromness through the sheltered waters of Scapa Flow. This northern Mediterranean, surrounded by the Mainland of Orkney and its South Isles, has been at the centre of Orkney's history for a thousand years. The Flow was the anchorage of the Royal Navy in both world wars. Here the *Vanguard* blew up (1917) and the *Royal Oak* was torpedoed (1939). From Scapa Flow the Grand Fleet left to engage the Germans at Jutland in 1916, and in it three years later the captured German Navy (72 ships totalling a quarter of a million tons) scuttled itself. On its east side, the massive Churchill Barrier, which helped at last to make Scapa Flow safe from attack by submarines, links by road five islands, one of which, Lamb Holm, has a moving reminder of the Italian prisoners-of-war who spent lonely years working on the Barrier causeways. This memorial (which the repatriated prisoners left in the care of the people of Orkney, and which has over 10,000 visitors each year) is a lovingly designed and exquisitely decorated chapel made entirely from Nissen huts and scrap materials. The spirit of its builders was humbler, and more Christlike, than that of the Norse king Olav Tryggvason, who captured an Orkney earl at the opposite side of the Flow in 995 and compelled him, at the point of the sword, to accept Christianity. The Norwegians of Orkney's classical period, brave men though they were — like the crusaders who sailed from Scapa to the Holy Land in the middle of the twelfth century, fighting and plundering as they rounded Spain and passed into the Tyrrhenian Sea — were not conscious of any conflict between piety and piracy. The owners of vessels wrecked on the shores of Orkney in more recent times are sometimes doubtful if the distinction has yet been understood; although the gallantry of the Longhope lifeboatmen, who were lost when attempting a rescue in mountainous seas in March 1969, is an assurance that in Orkney human lives are sacred and to be saved at any cost.

An adventurous way to see Orkney is to board a motor launch which plies from John o' Groats to St Margaret's Hope in South Ronaldsay for the greater part of the summer, following much the same route across the Pentland Firth as the almost mythical John o' Groat and succeeding ferrymen used. During the period when the 'short sea route', as it is sometimes called, is in operation, connecting buses carry travellers over the Barrier causeways to the Mainland, the chief island of the group, which has at various times had as its name Hrossey, Meginland and Pomona, the latter a romantic but errant name that one must never use. This large island covers 129 square miles and separates completely Orkney's South Isles from its more ragged and far-flung North Isles. Not only does the Mainland contain Orkney's two towns, Kirkwall and Stromness, but three-quarters of the county's population. From it, passenger and cargo boats, as well as small aeroplanes, link the outlying islands, and their isolation is further reduced by the weekly newspaper *The Orcadian* and the comparatively new local radio station *Radio Orkney*.

For nearly half-a-century this island county has had as the last part of its motto *Mare Amicus*, 'The Sea our Friend'. This was peculiarly apt when various parts of the islands made a reasonable livelihood from herring fishing, and when white fishing was pursued for home consumption. But it is now (apart from the true islander's undying love of the ocean and his gratitude for the Gulf Stream whose warm current tempers what would otherwise be a sub-Arctic climate) a somewhat ambivalent phrase. It is true that the encircling waters have given Orkney the insularity which has permitted it to maintain its quiet habit of life, and to preserve certain of its traditions. The same insularity has allowed the county, in a period of local government change, to have its own all-purpose authority, the Orkney Islands Council, with special powers voted to it by Parliament. The exercise of these powers has enabled it to cope with the demands of oil prospectors, to control extensive industrial developments, and to deal with changes in Orkney's economy which gather increasing momentum.

But the sea as a friend is an idea of more qualified appeal in days when the herring have disappeared northwards, when trawlers have denuded fish stocks, and when Orkney's major industry, farming, is crippled by the high freight rates of ships which bring in seeds, manures, implements and food for humans and animals, and which take away the islands' chief export, beef cattle. Mainland farmers and merchants pay a single freight, but farmers and men of business in the other islands, who normally buy and sell through local traders and in markets on the Mainland, are penalized by double freight. This is one cause of the serious loss of population experienced by such pleasant and fertile islands as Stronsay and Sanday, not to speak of some smaller islands. Another cause is the necessity for island children to go to a hostel in Kirkwall to continue their secondary education at the Grammar School there. A further break with their native islands must be made when the more able pupils go to university in Aberdeen, Edinburgh or elsewhere. Few indeed are the young people who return to their island homes. Most of those who do are boys to whom an academic or business life does not appeal, and who have farming in their blood. For the girls, always more profoundly affected by modern trends, there is less likelihood of going back. To them the remoter islands offer a mode of existence they no longer accept, without the compensation of jobs they would enjoy doing. They marry on the Mainland, almost as soon as they have closed their school-books, or become nurses, typists or shopgirls. There are small islands on which a single girl of marriageable age is seldom seen; in others there may be as many as fifteen boys to each girl. This disparity causes some lads to seek jobs outside their home islands; particularly when North Sea Oil, in the construction phase at least, offers what seem to be, to the unsophisticated, enviable rewards. There is an exception to the general trend, showing that job opportunities within the islands are desperately important. Westray, with at present a thriving fish-processing factory, is keeping its young people, particularly girls, better than the other North Isles, and has a pre-school population of such buoyancy that the number of scholars in the local school may increase.

The vacuum created by loss of population in some islands is being partly filled, but in an odd way, for farms which come on the market are sometimes bought by outsiders at prices no local farmer would dream of paying, while derelict cottages are seized on by all types of immigrants, from professors to drop-outs, trying desperately to find a way of life different from the urban one they have rejected. Some bring their skills with them. As a result one may find, working in old buildings surrounded by fields, electronic experts, potters, leather-workers, carvers, metal-workers, makers of grotesque gutta-percha masks, dealers in exotic books, artists, musicians, as well as people to whom work has come to be an unacceptable anachronism. Alongside these immigrants exist the ordinary Orcadians. Apart from the busy and prosperous full-time farmers, numbers of country people supplement their incomes by doing roadwork, fish processing, tangle gathering, machine knitting, car repairing, and other things as unexciting and practical; but basically they depend on the land, which in Orkney still offers greater rewards than in any other of the Scottish islands.

It has taken centuries to make the Orkney Islands as productive and fertile as they are now. Although always noted for the amount of grain they were able to grow, and which they exported to neighbouring Shetland, Norway, and the mainland of Scotland, they were agriculturally static, tied to the run-rig system, and harried by Scottish overlords and their rapacious underlings. A low standard of living, and a population at one time twice as big as it is now, forced people to leave the islands; so, for a long time, men sought employment in the Navy, in the service of the Hudson's Bay Company (in which several became famous), and in the Davis Strait whalers. Farming was grossly underrated as a means of livelihood until the kelp industry, made possible by the great masses of seaweed flung on the island coasts, suddenly faced fierce and crippling competition after the 1820s. Its collapse caused landlords, for their own survival no less than that of their tenants, to take up farming seriously and scientifically.

It was then that the latent productiveness of great portions of the Orkney land was appreciated. Efficient farming almost became a religion. Men, who had seemed indolent and lethargic at a time when no amount of enterprise or labour could benefit them, became as tenants, and much later (in the 1920s) as owner-occupiers, utterly devoted to their farms, producing with immense toil rich crops from what had been rough moorland and hill. In a century the brown heath became a variegated patchwork of roots, grass and grain, covered by cattle which were readily bought by dealers and southern farmers. Six thousand horses, glossy and vigorous, spent their energies year after year in extending the acreage of arable land. A multitude of poultry contributed 70,000,000 eggs a year, and a million pounds sterling, to the local economy.

After the second world war the tractor ousted the horse, and land hitherto untilled on hill-top and moor became clothed in rich sward. But poultry, the house-wife's main source of ready money, could not compete with the rising cost of feeding stuff and disappeared. This loss, which is still keenly felt, has not been adequately compensated for by various light industries which have since been introduced. The multicoloured pattern of the fields has almost gone, for farmers have discovered that in their northern climate, with its long summer daylight, grass is a more profitable crop than grain; so the countryside in summer is an expanse of almost monotonous verdure, constantly being converted into silage or placed in halage towers which are marring, along with huge, badly designed steadings, the appear-ance of the countryside. It comes as a surprise to the person who expected to find brown moorland, dirt roads, and the minimum of machinery, to discover 530 miles of well-surfaced highways and agricultural roads, and to learn that Orkney possesses more farm imple-ments and motor-cars than practically any comparable area of Britain or Europe.

Over five thousand cars, and the mobility they give, together with the opportunities for a more sophisti-cated social life now provided in the towns of Kirkwall and Stromness, or even in small island villages, help to ensure that former patterns of living are discarded. One result is that the young people of Orkney and many of their elders drink spirits far too frequently and with a strange unwisdom. But up to now the old values and standards of behaviour have been surprisingly tenacious; and the Orkney character, beautifully suggested in many of the faces which appear in this book, will be a long time a-dying . . . or so we fervently believe.

The Orkney character is not easy to define. Mingled Norse and Lowland Scottish blood, which pre-dominates, may still have in it traces of Pictish chief or Lappish thrall, of Highland immigrant, shipwrecked sailor or Red Indian squaw. North Ronaldsay is tradi-tionally supposed to have been a place of exile for Covenanters, as one or two Scottish surnames might seem to testify. Westray is convinced that survivors of the Armada settled on the island, and that even today their Latin features occasionally recur. South Ronaldsay has surnames which are suggestive of the flat fields of Caithness and the dales of Sutherland.

After centuries during which the more forceful sought new opportunities abroad, the Orcadian of today is by nature a peaceful man, disposed to rate 'inoffensive-ness' as the cardinal virtue. His feeling may be illus-trated by the words of an islander who said, after a visit to Eastern Europe, 'There were far too many people carrying guns. If there is a heaven, we have it here in Orkney.'

Then the Orcadian has clever, adaptable hands, used to busying themselves with a hundred different tasks. Usually he is as matter-of-fact as his northern ancestors, and seldom poetical, although he could, a generation ago, speak a local dialect full of telling similes and metaphors. Religion sits lightly on his shoulders, even if he is officially a churchman. Of mysticism he knows nothing, although it may be replaced to some small degree by a deep, inarticulate love of his islands, which is seldom allowed to show. This innate passion for Orkney, and for the things that belong to its peace, rose recently to fever heat when it seemed that uranium mining in a corridor stretching from the town of Stromness to the Atlantic coast at Yesnaby might destroy urban amenity, good agricultural land and some of the finest cliff scenery in the islands, as well as endangering the health of everyone on the Mainland. On this single issue, the native Orkneymen, who has not risen in his thousands since the battle of Summerdale in 1529 — the last on Orkney soil — is prepared to fight to the death.

The emphasis placed on food and hospitality is one of the most outstanding Orkney traditions, going back in time to the Norse farmers' obligatory 'neighbourhood ale' — a feast that followed harvest — and persisting through centuries when periods of famine caused people to share what they had with famishing strangers. The laden table in an Orkney farmhouse is still a wonderful sight, delightful or devastating to a visitor to the degree that he has already been entertained by determined hosts. Orcadians are probably seen at their best at harvest-homes or weddings, when they lose their shyness and relax, conscious of the community of goodwill that these traditional occasions generate. An Orkney wedding may have up to 300 guests, all of whom will slake their thirst and honour the bride by drinking from the 'bride's cog', a beautifully fashioned tub-shaped vessel filled with a special mixture of hot ale, spices and spirits. The feeling of participation in such an event is such that, in one island at least, invitations to weddings are sometimes given to the whole community by a notice in the grocery van. It may be mentioned as another instance of a fully integrated community that in many places — in Kirkwall invariably — funeral notices are posted in shop windows. Scores of cars may follow the hearse carrying some unassuming, but well liked, individual to the local cemetery.

Except for the young people, Orcadians seldom indulge in strenuous sports. There is plenty of work on the farms to stretch the muscles; so rock-climbing, hiking, and sea-angling, for which there are excellent opportunities, are mostly left to energetic visitors. The local man prefers a day's fishing on one of the fine trout lochs (free of charge to all), a sail in his boat in the evening, or a run in his car on a Sunday afternoon to see how work is progressing in half-a-dozen parishes. In addition, he can constantly refresh his soul by gazing over blue firths to the neighbouring islands, or by watching the birds which wheel in myriads round their ancestral cliffs.

When the dearth of strenuous sports is mentioned, an exception must be made. While Christmas and New Year's Day are celebrated nearly everywhere in the conventional way, the men of Kirkwall, divided into groups called *Uppies* and *Doonies*, with the Market Cross in front of St Magnus Cathedral as their starting-off point, spend the afternoons of both festivals in endeavouring to carry a cork-filled leather ball to the extreme limit of their territory — the head of the town for the *Uppies*, the harbour for the *Doonies*. Windows and doors in the narrow old streets are barricaded. The game, always involving torn clothes, many bruises, and sometimes broken ribs, may take hours, and if the ball should reach the harbour some of the hardier contestants follow it into the ice-cold water. An American observer has called the game 'mass mayhem'.

In Stromness, a gala week in July, now over a quarter of a century old, has become a tradition, attracting crowds of islanders. But the great gathering of the year is the County Show in Kirkwall, an agricultural shop-window for the islands which has replaced the former Lammas Market, and which collects together in a single park one-third of the population of Orkney. Interest in agriculture is responsible, too, for the continuance of Orkney's only other calendar event of traditional importance, the Boys' Ploughing Match in the island of South Ronaldsay. Boys, with splendidly fashioned miniature ploughs, compete in 'ploughing' a flat, firm patch of damp sand, with adult judges and crowds of spectators critically viewing their efforts. At an earlier stage the ploughmen meet in the village hall at St. Margaret's Hope to have their ploughs judged, and to march around the square with their 'horses', which are girls gorgeously dressed in costumes that dazzle the eye. Basic to the dress are hames, collars, bridles, fetlocks, silver-edged shoes and so on; but after that fancy takes over, and anything that sparkles, along with ribbons and bells, is added. The event has taken place at Easter from time out of mind, growing from small beginnings to its present magnificence; but, sad to say, the desire to cater for tourists has caused it to be transferred to the month of August, regardless of custom and of the period when ploughing would normally be in progress.

This concession to commercialism does not mean that the average Orcadian has little regard for his traditions and history. Orkney was the first county in Scotland to appoint a county archivist to look after its historical documents, running into scores of thousands. These are housed in the County Library in Kirkwall, an institution which, in various forms, has had a history covering three centuries, and which has rejoiced in recent times in a book issue of nearly twice the national average. One of its major commitments is a Family Book Service which sends boxes of books to individual families in all the outer islands. Another much appreciated service is performed by the mobile library van, which penetrates to every corner of the Mainland. The history and natural history of Orkney is given visual expression in two well conducted museums. There is a comparatively new one in Kirkwall, occupying Tankerness House, a beautiful old family mansion, and a much older one in Stromness, which has grown up with Orkney Natural History Society, founded in 1837. The Kirkwall museum concerns itself largely with the history and prehistory of the islands and with changing modes of life, while the Stromness Museum has concentrated more on natural history and maritime matters. A farm museum in the heart of the countryside is to be set up as soon as money becomes available. Stromness may have by the time this book appears, or soon afterwards, a remarkable art centre based on a unique collection of twentieth century abstract art given to Orkney as a token of appreciation of what the islands have meant to the donar over many years.

Although practically treeless, and possessing very quiet landscapes (blotted here and there, it must be admitted, with such things as car graveyards, ugly council houses and unsightly private ones, together with some untidy farmsteads), Orkney gains its loveliness from its fine coastal scenery, rolling, wine-coloured hills, and constant views of a sea so blue in summer as to be almost unbelievable. From its wide sky pours the wonderful northern light that artists try, almost hopelessly, to get into their picture. They keep on trying, nevertheless; for there are many amateur artists in the county. Thus, the islands are seldom without an exhibition of someone's local paintings. Certain of these artists have considerable skill, and it should be remembered that the famous painter and Queen's Limner, Stanley Cursiter R.S.A., who died in 1976, was an Orcadian.

If painting is an art much practised, so is writing, especially of studies in local history. Few counties can boast a collection of the value and variety of that housed in the Orkney Room of Kirkwall Library, where there are 5,000 books and pamphlets concerned with matters which have a more or less direct bearing on Orkney's life and history, including a splendid collection of Northern texts, sagas and heroic histories, works on archaeology and folklore, and scholarly volumes on numerous aspects of Scandinavian life and thought. The specifically Orcadian part of this collection includes a surprising number of books written and printed in Orkney. For well over a century there has been a tradition of printing local books within the islands, and some fine examples of typography and book production have come from presses in Kirkwall and Stromness. The best philological, sociological and historical works have been produced by local scholars. Nor has Orkney been behind in literature. Three excellent writers have dominated Orkney literature this century: Edwin Muir, Eric Linklater and George Mackay Brown. But behind these leaders have stood numbers of men and women who have contributed significantly to poetry, narrative writing, and belles-lettres.

The time has not yet come for native musicians to interpret their landscape and way of life in sophisticated music, but a well-known modern musician, Peter Maxwell Davies, who lives and works in a cottage in the lovely deserted township of Rackwrek in Hoy, is doing that for them. Meanwhile, plenty of fiddlers and accordionists practise, enjoy, and frequently compose their reels, strathspeys and other traditional tunes, or write folk-songs with local themes.

Orkney history, geography and sociology now have some place in the curricula of all island schools, and, as far as time allows, are taught at a high level in the secondary schools. This is good, for a considerable proportion of Orcadians are avid for information about their native islands. They were starved of such information in past times; and today their interest is further stimulated by an instinct that in a generation or two their way of life may have changed considerably. There will be substantial gains, perhaps, but certainly losses that a people excessively conscious of its closely-knit identity will find it difficult to accept.

Up to last century, the average Orcadian, even the most intelligent student, knew little about the history of Orkney. It was accepted that the Stewart earls — Earl Robert Stewart, who received a grant of the Orkney lands from his half-sister Mary Queen of Scots in 1564, and his son Patrick (the 'Black Pate' of local tradition) who was beheaded in Edinburgh in 1615 — had been tyrants of the first magnitude, and had introduced to the islands, in addition to the splendid palaces they built at Birsay and Kirkwall, a numerous company of their Lowland Scottish friends, some of them much more cruel than their patrons. These despots gradually wrested the land from the freeholders, or *udallers*, who held it. Certain of the newcomers became great land-owners, who imposed on the peasantry a state of existence little short of serfdom. To some extent this story of usurpation was simplified, and many of the allegations made against Earl Patrick as an individual

may have been unjust, but, looking back, the Orcadian was conscious of a long night of tyranny, dispelled by a slow dawn in the last half of the nineteenth century. Anything that happened before 1468, when the Orkney Islands were mortgaged to Scotland by Christian I of Denmark and Norway as a dowry for his daughter Margaret, wife of James III of Scotland, was vaguely understood. It was long hoped that they would be redeemed in cash, as King Christian had led the Norwegians, who really owned them, to believe; but if Christian or his successors made any determined efforts to get the islands back, the Scots always managed to frustrate them. There is little enthusiasm in Orkney, even at this late date, for a Scottish parliament. People feel that the individuals who would dominate it would differ only in class and situation from the tyrants of past centuries.

With the nineteenth century, and the growth of historical enlightenment, the older Norwegian links with Orkney began to be examined. In 1844 a remarkable Orcadian, Samuel Laing of Papdale, who had done much to improve Orkney farming and who had built up herring fishing in the North Isles into a considerable industry, published for the first time in English Snorri Sturluson's *Heimskringla*, the Sagas of the Norse Kings, a text so good that it is still used in the *Everyman* edition. Laing's writings influenced such contemporaries as Thomas Carlyle and John Stuart Mill; but Orkney itself did not gain a realisation of its Norwegian past until our own island saga, *The Orkneyinga Saga* written in Iceland in the thirteenth century, was translated in 1873, and again in 1894.

This saga told the story of the Orkney Earls and their doings from about 900 A.D. to about 1200 A.D. Its contents were analysed and popularised by a band of enthusiastic local historians. Gradually, Orkney got used to the idea that it had had a heroic age, when such powerful Orkney Earls as Thorfinn the Mighty had added to their island dominions the Western Islands, extensive tracts of Scotland, and part of Ireland. In those days, people realised, Orkney was at the hub, not the perimeter, of a northern empire. The part of the *Saga*, however, which made the greatest impression was that which explained the siting of such a great building as St Magnus Cathedral in the little town of Kirkwall (first mentioned as a hamlet in 1046), and which told the story of the two earls, canonised as saints, who inspired and founded that church. The story is retold in practically every account of Orkney, and at length in J. Storer Clouston's *A History of Orkney* and John Mooney's *St Magnus Earl of Orkney*, so need only be summarized here.

Earl Thorfinn's grandsons, Hakon Paulsson and Magnus Erlendsson, together ruled Orkney in the early twelfth century. Hakon, a man of courage and a typical Norseman, was the antithesis of Magnus, a man born out of his time, who became more and more absorbed in problems of personal sanctity, and who was possibly as idiosyncratic in his relations with his cousin as in his ideas of how Orkney should be ruled. Magnus's Christian conscience, seemingly over-developed, and Hakon's robust and possibly ruthless practicality came into conflict to such an extent that a peace meeting was arranged in April 1117 on the island of Egilsay. Hakon's followers took advantage of the situation, gathered a stronger force than Magnus, and, with the Christian Earl in their power, insisted on his death.

The Magnus part of the *Saga* story, written by priests, dramatises the event and emphasises the almost unbelievable love and forbearance of Magnus, but an Egilsay tradition existing to this day points to a simple, quick and undramatic murder. Whatever the truth, it is clear that Magnus by his life had made a strong impression on the rough islanders, so that when he was buried in his grandfather's church, called Christchurch, in Birsay, people afflicted by sickness and mental distress came to his grave from all parts of Orkney and Shetland, and miraculous cures were reported.

Popular belief in Magnus's sanctity became too strong to be repudiated, and he was canonised. When his nephew, Rognvald Kolson in Norway, a claimant to part of the Orkney earldom, found difficulty in asserting his right, he vowed that if he was successful in achieving his purpose he would build a cathedral in honour of Magnus in the town of Kirkwall. This vow may have been made in part to gain the aid of a remarkable island bishop, William the Old, and to enlist the sympathy of the Orcadians, but it was made in good faith and was loyally kept. As soon as Rognvald became Earl he started building the Cathedral, employing Norman masons, and gathering revenues to make sure that it should be, in his own words, 'the marvel and glory of the North.' This, in the course of centuries, it became; and so it remains: a red sandstone church, beautifully proportioned, and adorned mainly by the vigorous simplicity of its design and the magnificent character of its workmanship. In it the relics of both Magnus and Rognvald repose. It remained the property of the Norse and Scoto-Norse Earls who succeeded Rognvald, until it was given to the town of Kirkwall by James III. Coveted by the Church, the fabric has remained in secular hands, and is now the responsibility of the Orkney Islands Council.

The Cathedral has a perfect setting. The grey streets of the old town wend their way towards it, and it is surrounded by interesting old buildings, including the ruins of the palaces of earl and bishop. It has a wonderful voice in the form of a sweet-toned Willis organ, recently rebuilt, which is used both for Sunday worship and week-day recitals of classical and modern music. Every evening, at one minute past eight o'clock, its curfew bell, one of the most venerable of the older voices of Kirkwall, rings for five minutes. The Sunday Call to Worship, played by a single ringer on three bells dating from 1528, is unique.

Rognvald has a place in Orkney history distinct from his founding of the Cathedral and his various Viking adventures, in that he gathered to his court in Kirkwall poets and musicians. With one of the scalds, an

Icelander, he composed a text-book for poets *Hattalykill*, and some of his poems, composed on crusade, are included in *The Orkneyinga Saga*. A Norse literary tradition developed in the islands, and was given splended expression some decades later by Bishop Bjarni Kolbeinson (born in the island of Wyre, on the very farm where another great Orkney poet, Edwin Muir, was brought up.) Bjarni's *Lay of the Jomsvikings* is still remembered. He is looked on as the founder of Kirkwall Grammar School, which is thus older than Eton College.

Just as nineteenth century Orkney became aware of its Norse past — realising that many of its surnames, numbers of its traditions, and the great majority of its place-names are Norse — so twentieth century Orkney has been gradually introduced by archaeologists to a prehistory rich almost beyond comprehension. Those henge monuments the Ring of Brodgar and the Standing Stones of Stenness, and the chambered tomb of Maeshowe, had been long known: they were symbolic of the ancient origins of human settlement on the islands and gave vague clues to its pattern. But the past half-century has shown that Orkney is covered by at least a thousand prehistoric sites, in all probability by many more, and that some of these are of as great importance as the classic monuments. The remarkable thing about many of them is their completeness: they are not mere indications in the soil, or little heaps of stone whose original form is difficult to visualise — far from it! Two houses at the Knap of Howar, in the island of Papa Westray, although over five thousand years old, are of wall height, as are one or two houses in the rather younger settlement of Skara Brae. Chambered and stalled cairns, found during the modern period, are wonderfully complete; and the Iron Age brochs so far uncovered (two or three out of a hundred that lie hidden in the earth or only partially revealed) are of massive proportions. Neolithic monuments, and the brochs, were the first to be explored in depth: they were most easy to identify. During the last twenty

years, however, Norse settlements have been excavated at several places, and in the past decade, with increasingly interesting results, Bronze Age farms, with fields still showing plough marks, and houses complete with cooking-places, in which long water-filled troughs were heated with red-hot stones, have come to light. By the use of radio-carbon dating and other modern techniques, prehistory is assuming something of the sureness and authority of recorded history, and no more exciting field than Orkney for archaeological investigation could be imagined.

This is partly due to the treelessness of the islands. In more favoured climatic situations ancient wooden structures have completely disappeared. But Orkney has been fortunate in possessing a type of building stone which can be lifted in smooth pieces with straight edges. On some coasts the sea has quarried this stone ready for use. The flagstones vary in thickness and in size, so as to be equally suitable for walls or roofs. Here and there, the stones are so massive that 'standing stones' of twenty feet and more were easily obtained. This extraordinary adaptable material was available to the earliest settlers, and has been used by Orcadians during five millenia.

It used to be an aphorism of local antiquaries that the Stone Age lasted in Orkney until the nineteenth century. They were giving playful expression to the fact that the old Orkney croft-house contained the minimum of wood and metal. A few spars found on the beach, or taken from one of the many ships that were wrecked on the treacherous coasts, supported the stone flags of the roof. The floor was also of stone. Some of the 'furniture' was reminiscent of Skara Brae: stones set on edge to support a flat flagstone made a *bink*, or table; another such stone let into a rounded recess in the wall (the *sae-bink*) supported the *sae*, or water tub; beds were frequently stone recesses let into a thickened portion of the wall and 'curtained' in front by slabs of stone at either side. These beds were called *neuk-beds*. There might be a stone shelf for the *quern*, or stone grinding-mill. In the chief room, the *firehouse*, a peat fire was built against a stone wall in the middle of the floor. From this the smoke curled upwards and along the rafters to escape through a hole in the roof. In the smoke, to help 'cure' the simple food, hung lines of drying fish, pieces of mutton and pork, and perhaps a wild duck or goose. Such foods, with oatmeal, beremeal and milk, provided a healthy, if spartan, diet.

Chairs, and most of the farm baskets and creels (called *kaisies* or *cubbies* according to type) were made of straw, a material adapted most cleverly to scores of uses, including the thatching of the flagged roofs. Some comfort was given to rather primitive homes by the abundance of peats available.

The Orkney of yesterday, in which dwelling-house, cow byre, stable and barn were built as a single long unit or divided by a narrow passage called a *kloss*, has long since disappeared, but an example of a *firehouse* with a central fire may be seen at Kirbister (Birsay). Partly ruined houses with *neuk beds*, stone *aamries*, or presses, and other domestic features of stone, exist at Winksetter (Harray), Mossetter (Rendall) and Langalour (Firth).

Some gracious examples of vernacular building of a larger sort used to exist, most of them the homes of landlords or ministers, but these — apart from a few isolated examples, of which the finest is Skaill in Sandwick, a stone's-throw from Skara Brae — have been allowed to fall into ruin or unskilfully modernised. How pleasingly Orkney stone could be utilised, however, and how charmingly it could it into the landscape, is exemplified by the town of Stromness, whose old buildings (sometimes rising sheer from the sea), its dozens of stone jetties, and its stone-paved streets, make it, as the architect and writer James Stevens Curl has said, 'a national treasure.' Along with the older parts of Kirkwall, it has been designated a conservation area, and recognised as 'outstanding' by the Historic Buildings Council for Scotland.

Several societies exist to care for Orkney's architec-tural features, its wild-life and its traditions. There are also a number of nature reserves, some of them isolated islands (like Copinsay, which has been acquired as a memorial to the late James Fisher); for the bird life of the county, as concentrated particularly on its sea-cliffs and moors, is a source of pleasure to resident and visitor alike, as is the wealth of wild flowers in summer. The flowers include the somewhat rare *Primula scotica*. Some absentees, alas, from our flowering plants are Harebell, Purple Loosetrife, Anemone, Globe Flower, and the water-lilies; but we have the Pyramid Bugle, Oyster Plant and Mountain Sorrel. In places the proliferation of flowers, such as Marsh Marigold and Sea Pink, gives beauty to otherwise featureless situations.

Both birds and flowers have had to make some retreat before an advancing agriculture, but stern economics make Orcadians thankful that cattle have increased from around 39,000 in 1935 to something like 98,000 today. Sheep, which reached a peak of 102,000 in 1961, have fallen to a current figure of 75,000. Most people are bored by statistics, but with the resources they possess, Orcadians are proud that their gross annual county product is around £16,000,000, with agriculture accounting for well over half that figure. There are two whisky distilleries, bringing in £3,300,000 of our gross product, while we depend on tourism for around £1,500,000. These figures, broadly correct as this summary of Orkney life is being written, vary from time to time; and the economy will be considerably affected as the present oil installations, and those which may yet be built, come into full production.

Orkney has accepted North Sea oil with considerable caution and not a few reservations. While it is unlikely that this mammoth industry, with its almost unparalleled capital expenditure, tremendous threat to amenity, and promise of increasing financial reward, will disturb Orkney quite as traumatically as the neighbouring islands of Shetland, the effect of future discoveries on people and landscape, and the long term damage of inevitable oil-spills to the marine and bird life of Orkney, cannot be estimated.

The photographs in this book, which picture the face of Orkney more candidly and yet more sympathetically than any writer can, will show that up to now the county has managed to take its place in the modern world — in respect of its own natural resources and in its assimilation into its social and domestic life of the modern amenities it can best use — without losing too many of the customs and traditions which give it a special character and ethos. The natural environment, and the inborn attitudes of the Orkney people, will help in their different ways to preserve our peculiarly satisfying kind of life for years to come, unless commercial and political pressures, and ruthless exploitation of the soil and the minerals which underlie it, are too strong for us to resist. Such a book as this can do much to strengthen our resistance to exterior forces that might otherwise daunt our spirits; for it shows on page after page precious things that could so easily be destroyed. It may seem a strange and arrogant thing to say, but, in an age which is becoming increasingly materialistic and devoid of character and singularity, the loss of a way of life as rare in quality as that of Orkney would be a loss to the world.

1. *Kirkwall Airport.*

2. View from Wideford Hill, near Kirkwall.

3. *The Bay of Skaill, West Mainland.*

4. *Hoy from Stromness.*

5. *Scapa Flow from Stromness. British naval anchorage during two wars, and graveyard of the 1st World War German Fleet.*

6. *Sea cliffs at Birsay, West Mainland.*

7. *A Mainland farm.*

8. *Windbreck, Graemsay. The trough is half a buoy from World War II submarine nets with guarded Scapa Flow.*

9. *Hay being brought indoors for the winter feeding of cattle, Shapinsay.*

10. *Cattle are the mainstay of Orkney's economy.*

11. *Kirkwall Auction Market.*

12. A recaptured runaway cow in calf is dragged back to Kirkwall slaughterhouse.
The cow would have suffered giving birth to her calf due to complications.

13. *Kirkwall slaughterhouse.*

14. *Feeding the pigs, Burray.*

15.   Feeding the hens, North Ronaldsay.

16.   *A barn interior.*

17. *Hen plucking.*

18. *A Graemsay crofter.*

19. *Cleaning up after milking.*

20. *Milking time on a Mainland dairy farm.*

21. *Butter being made at Claymore*
Creamery, Kirkwall.

22.   *Wind can be a problem in Orkney.*

23. *Sheep being brought from their grazing on the small island of Copinsay for sale in Kirkwall.*

24. *North Ronaldsay sheep are a special breed which live outside a dyke built around the island. They are communally owned, and eat mainly seaweed.*

25.   A Mainland farmer.

26.   *At the Dounby Agricultural Show.*

27.   *New farm machinery always attracts a lot of attention at the shows.*

28. *The annual sheepdog trials.*

29. The County Ploughing Match.

30. *Blockships sunk during wartime to protect the naval anchorage at Scapa Flow can still be seen in places.*

31. *The Churchill Barriers were built by Italian prisoners during the 2nd World War.*

32. *A part-time lobster fisherman,*
Papa Westray.

33. *Boiling crabs at Orkney Fisher-men's Society Ltd., a co-operative in Stromness. The cooked meat is packaged and exported. Lobsters are flown out live.*

34.   *Diving for clams in Scapa Flow.*

35. *Fish processing, Westray.*

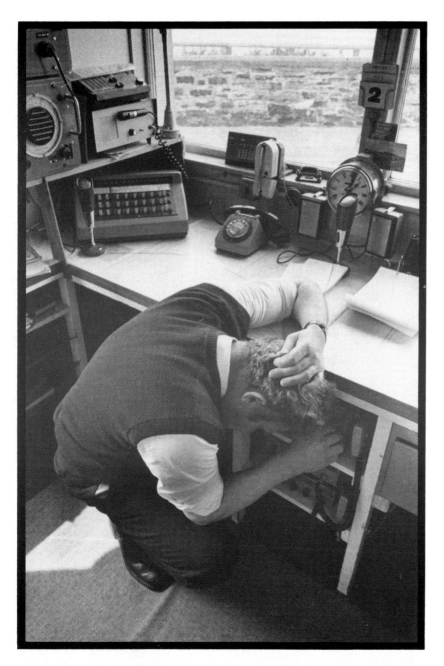

36. *Kirkwall coastguard.*

37. *Fishing boat in a gale in Scapa Flow.*

38.   *Stromness Life-boat.*

39. 'The Islander', one of the cargo boats serving the North Isles, is helped back to Kirkwall by the 'Clytus' and Kirkwall Life-boat after damaging her propeller.

40.   *Albert Kirkpatrick, skipper of the 'Hoy Head' which served the South Isles for many years. She was replaced by the 'Lyrawa Bay' in 1977.*

41. *Unloading the weekly cargo, North Ronaldsay.*

42. *Duncan's Boatyard, Burray, a family firm which has specialised in building wooden inshore fishing boats.*

43. *Orcantic Ltd., Hatston, make fibreglass hulls and other fibreglass products.*

44. *Making a lobster creel in spare time.*

45.   *Lilla Crisp and her brother-in-law Ernie, Shapinsay. Ernie died in 1978.*

46. *Willie Thompson of Neven, North Ronaldsay, a retired seaman, paints pictures of old sailing ships for pleasure.*

47. *Annie Thompson of Greenspot, North Ronaldsay, knits and crochets for Isle of Sanday Knitters Ltd.*

48. *A typical island airfield.*

49. *Loganair serve the outer islands from the Mainland of Orkney with Islander aircraft which carry nine passengers.*

50.   *Most islands have their own doctor.*

51. New shoes bought by mail order, Papa Westray.

52. *Island shops stock a wide variety of goods from Wellington boots to cornflakes. This is the shop at Hullion, Rousay.*

53. *Island shops also tend to be social centres.*

54. *Isaac Moar, Postmaster, Hoy.*

55. *Kirkwall Post Office.*

56. *Shopping in Kirkwall.*

57. 'Just About Anything', a Kirkwall junk shop.

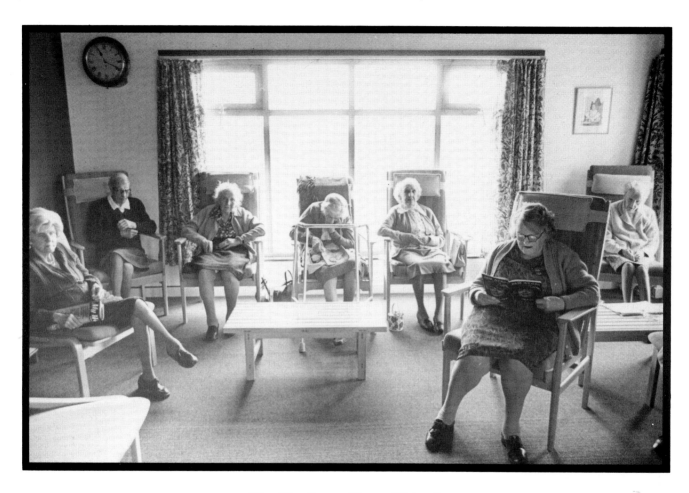

58. The County Home, Kirkwall.

59. *The late Ernest W. Marwick, folklorist, author, historian, with his wife Janette.*

60.   *Lord Birsay.*

61. *An island party.*

62. *Some islanders still depend on well water.*

63.   *Fay and son, incomers to Sanday.*

64.   *Council housing estate, Kirkwall.*

65. *A Mainland household.*

66. *St. Magnus Cathedral.*

67. *A wedding at the cathedral.*

68. *Through depopulation, Graemsay school is one of the smallest in Orkney.*

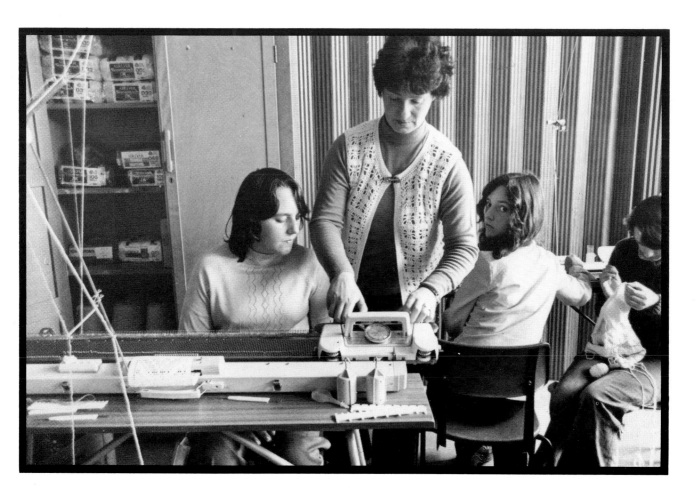

69.   Kirkwall Grammar School.

70. *Pupils from the outer islands attending Kirkwall Grammar School stay at this hostel in Kirkwall.*

71. *Playing snooker, Kirkwall.*

72.   *At a Rugby Club fair.*

73. *Laying out peat to dry for winter fuel.*

74. *The Queens Hotel bar, Kirkwall.*

75. *Flower Show, Kirkwall.*

76. *Jo Grimond has for many years been M.P. for Orkney and Shetland.*

77. *Howie Firth, S.N.P. candidate for Orkney and Shetland, talks to performers after compering a show. Howie is now senior producer of Radio Orkney.*

78. *Mary Wards is one of the few people in Orkney who still spin wool.*

79. *Many Orcadians are fine craftsmen in their spare time. Mr Brown of Hackland makes the traditional Bride's Cogs and the occasional spinning wheel.*

80. *Most part-time home knitting is done by machine to supply flourishing local knitting firms which export widely.*

81.   *Some women still do hand knitting.*

82. *Making traditional Orkney chairs,*
Kirkwall.

83. *Sheepskin curing, Mainland. A small-scale cottage industry.*

84. *A pottery at 'Banks', Rousay. A number of craft potteries have started in Orkney during the 1970s.*

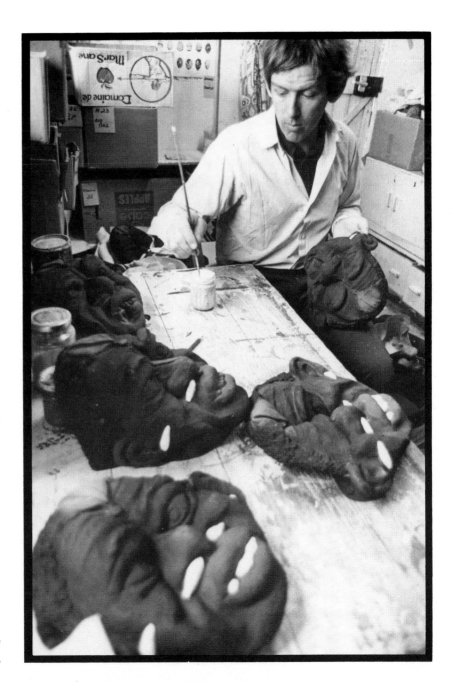

85. *A recently introduced rubber mask factory in Sanday.*

86. *There are two jewellery manu-*
facturers in Orkney, 'Ola M.
Gorie' shown here, and 'Ortak'.

87. *A retired coastguard, Harry Berry, lives in Hoy and paints life-boat rescues to raise funds for the Royal National Life-boat Institution.*

88. *The late Reynold Eunson, a Kirkwall wood-carver.*

89. *Cobbler, Kirkwall.*

90. *Tourism is a growing industry.*

91. *Tankerness House Museum, Kirkwall.*

92. *The main street in Stromness.*

93. *'Yard of Ale' competition, Stromness Shopping Week.*

94. *Stromness Shopping Week Fancy Dress Parade.*

95. *Drying fish in the sun, Stromness. This practice had all but died out.*

96. *The Neolithic settlement of Skara Brae.*

97. *The Ring of Brodgar.*

98. *Orkney frequently has beautiful sunrises and sunsets.*

99.   *A coffee evening in Tankerness House Gardens.*

100.   The traditional Boys' Ploughing Match, South Ronaldsay.

101.   *Enthusiastic support at the Kirkwall New Year Ba' Game.*

102. Delivering mail to a Mainland farm.

103. *Robertson's 'Orkney Fudge' Factory, Stromness.*

104. *Highland Park Distillery, Kirkwall.*

105. *Orkney Builders Ltd., Hatston, Kirkwall.*

106. *Walliwall Quarry, near Kirkwall.*

107. Road-work, Kirkwall.

108. *North Sea Oil Terminal, Flotta.*

109. *Many people travel daily from the Mainland of Orkney to work at Flotta Oil Terminal.*

110.   *Orkney farms are not always tidy.*

111. *A view from the Schoolmaster's house, Graemsay.*

112.   *Meeting of Orkney Scrambling Club.*

113.   'Midnight' Golf, Kirkwall.

114.   *Digging for 'spoots' or razorfish, a local delicacy, on the low spring tides.*

115.   *Trout fishing on the Harray Loch.*

116. *Orkney waters provide excellent sport for sea anglers.*

117.   *At the weigh-in of the John Player Sea Angling Competition, Stromness.*

118.   *Stromness Academy sailing lessons.*

119. *Model yacht racing at the Peerie Sea, Kirkwall.*

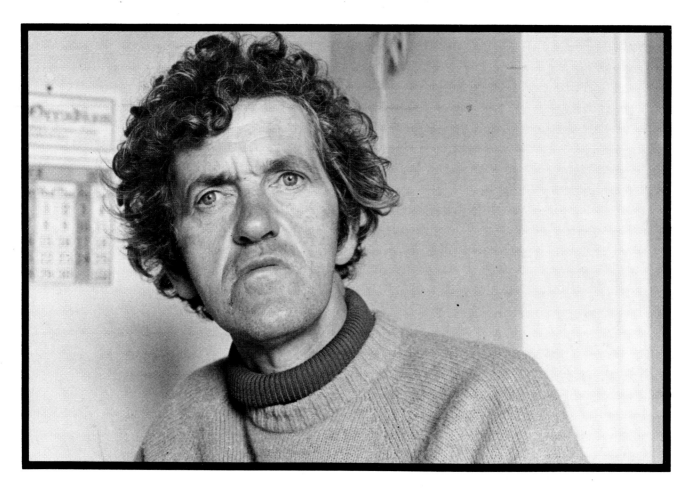

120. *George Mackay Brown, poet, short story writer and novelist.*

121.   *Wall decoration, Stromness.*

122.   *Orkney has a large seal population.*

123. *Stone slabs or 'flags' are readily available for building. Here on Westray they are used to reinforce fencing.*

124. Rackwick, Hoy.

125. *Betty Corrigal, a young Hoy woman who committed suicide in the early 19th century was not accepted for burial in consecrated ground, but buried in a lonely spot on the parish border. Her grave is tended by a sympahetic visitor.*

126.   *M.V. 'St. Ola', Orkney's daily link with the mainland of Scotland.*